PROMPTED.

Introduction

During the most difficult year I've faced, and with support and encouragement in unexpected places, the idea of *Prompted.* was born. After all, I had nothing to lose anymore. So, maybe being stripped of everything I knew was exactly what I needed to get me here, to bring these words to others in a tangible form. That space gave me the spark to put my fears aside so I could finally do the scary thing of publishing my first book, something I've been putting off for years. However, I do believe timing is everything. Consider this me dipping my toe into the pool of possibility.

Here you will find poems written based on prompts I was given by friends and loved ones, as well as myself.

Thank you for reading. <3

The front cover art was designed by Alex Ochoa.

Prompted.

ADRIANA OCHOA

Adriana Ochoa

In Hopes

The thing is, poetry,
These words, have always
Saved me.

When I literally
Had nothing to my name,
I still had my words, my brain.

Word by word,
Poem by poem,
I've found my way back
          (to myself).

So, while I may
Make a fool of myself
In the time I am making
          (something from nothing),

I hope you know
This isn't just an attempt
To save myself
          (it's in hopes it helps save you too).

<u>What Binds Us</u>

Whatever the world may bring us,
May we always have the love that
Found us, bound us, in the first place.
Because my death a thousand times
Could still be something beautiful
If your love is still what I come home to.

Wherever I find myself
Wherever I find you, my love,
May it be the reminder
That no matter where we go
I will carry you back with me.
Every time.
Every.
Time.

<u>First Sip of Coffee or Tea</u>

I know what heaven tastes like
Every morning when
I have my first sip of coffee.
When the balance of honey
To milk to cinnamon
Is just right,
The taste of the beans is
Enhanced with the heat.
The world is quiet then
My mind is quiet then.
There is just this warm bliss
As I wake up.

<u>Childhood Toys</u>

Skippy is the name
Of my first favorite toy.
She was a grey and brown cat
With specks of blue in her "fur."
A Beanie Baby, with the heart shaped tag.

I distinctly remember
Cuddling her for comfort, and
Pretending to be a mama cat
Grooming her child.
She was my comfort instead of a blanket.
She was my favorite
Before I grew up and cared about
Teddy bears boys got me.
Now she sits in a bag
With my Cabbage Patch doll, and
My other two favorite stuffed animals.
While the rest were let go long ago,
She still follows me to my new homes.
I have a piece of my childhood
Whenever I need to remember a time
When play was pure, and so was I.

<u>Social Anxiety</u>

My heart races
My palms itch invisibly,
But no amount of scratching
Calms the sensation.
Sweat then replaces the itch.

I cannot move my legs
I cannot move my body.
Simple tasks race in my head
And the guilt of not being able
To get past the fears in my head
Rises as I become more
Immobile.

I have to ask for help,
But it never seems like help.
I just ask for company.
Then suddenly,
Everything is easier,
The fears subside.
I am free.

<u>Fear of Losing a Relationship</u>

I stand at the edge
Of all that we've been
Seeing on the other side
All that we could be,
And I am frozen.
What if the words I speak
Are the ones that change us
Irrevocably.
What if my feelings
Mean that this may stop here.
But what if the cliff
That I stand on still has a path
To the other side that
Brings us to a new beginning
Together.
I can't breathe.
I see you.
I see me.
I see us.
Still,
There is the unspoken -
The elephant in the room.
We can't avoid this anymore.
Here I go off the edge...

An Overgrown Forest, But It's You Not Taking Care of Your Feelings

Trees, nothing but emerald trees
As far as the eye can see.
Quite a few are tall and scraping
Far above the younger trees,
That haven't had the opportunity
To meet the warmth of the sun, unencumbered.
On the floor,
There are brown leaves, dirt,
Fallen branches decomposing
With the moss that
Create the cool earth
Beneath such massive beauty.
How long have they been here,
My whole life?
Just a few years?
When did this grove become a forest,
When did the ferns become wild,
With plants that have grown
Bigger than me?
I place my palm on the trunk
Of the biggest, wisest looking tree.
Immediately, I snap my hand back.
Pain radiates through my hand
Into my chest.
What was that?

As tears prickle to my eyes,
A memory from childhood surfaces.
It was the first time I felt
Forgotten, unimportant, rejected.
How must this forest feel
If it's stored all the pain ever felt,
Then left to grow on its own,
Untouched by loving hands?
Uncared for, unseen for its beauty and
Its wisdom?

<u>A Return</u>

The magic is in the moment
You return to the heart
You also abandoned when
You were a child.

Yes, it hurt when everyone
Else walked away, but
It meant nothing until
You left it alone, too.

<u>What it Means to You to Be Happy</u>

Happiness is the comfort
Of my nightly routine of
Brewing tea, breathing, brushing my teeth,
Being alone with my thoughts.

Happiness is the freedom of
A morning with no commitments
But to worshipping the sun rays
That peak through my windows,
Praising me for making it
To another day in my own skin.

Happiness is when I realize,
Mid-laughter, how the people around me
Just want to support me the way
That I support them.

Happiness is fresh food with
The people I love as we tell
Our stories over the past few
Days, weeks, months.

Happiness is not having to hide
Who I am or the heart I have.

Happiness is my niece's laughter,
A nice drive with the windows down,
Grey skies and green earth.

Happiness is my community,
My sovereignty,
And everything that that ties us together-
Seeing the life I'm building,
And for once feeling like I matter,
That I belong.

Stretch Marks and Bodies

It's been so long since I've
Stopped and paid attention
To my body.
Look at these stretch marks,
Reminding me of the life I've lived.

This body has carried me
Through all of my darkest moments.
Here I stand,
With grace and grit, and
An unshakeable determination
To keep living.

I will never betray this body again,
For it has always supported me and
Kept me going,
Even when there were times
I didn't think it would.

What a thing of beauty,
To have something fighting for you
Always,
Always,
Always.

<u>Something You Struggle to Live Up To</u>

"Speak up. You have every right to
Advocate for yourself."
I firmly state these words
To anyone I know
Needs to hear them.
When it's my turn to
Not just hear them,
To also live by them,
I choke.
My throat closes,
My diaphragm stops.
Whispers and squeaks are
All you can hear.
Who is this child that's
Resurfaced when I need
The fire of my conviction and
My thunderous protection?
I deserve boundaries,
My justice, my voice,
Just as much as anyone else.
So why am I still convinced
I have not earned it?
As if you'd ever have to earn those.

Looking Back

As I look back at the rubble
I know this was never meant
To harden me,
It's quite the opposite.
I have softened.
There is no guard or walls anymore.
There is just my heart,
Timid and scared,
Looking back at me
Like a child that needs
Reassurance it is safe.
You are free, sweetheart.
I will keep you safe.

Tears of Peace

There is a weight lifted
From these worn shoulders
Every time a wave of tears
Warmly streams down my face and
Cools at the base of my neck.

A bittersweet relief that both
Loosens the grip around my heart
But sinks me deeper into emotion,
All to say we kept our promise.
We did exactly what we said we'd do.

There is peace knowing
You are somewhere playing
As the child you once were with the love
You more than deserved but never got.
There is peace in knowing you're not in pain.

It is over.

Taking My Power Back – Softly

I'm trying to find more balance
In a world that benefits
When you're off kilter.
I'm trying to dedicate myself more to
Softness, stillness, intentionality.
I've been accepting responsibility
For absolutely everyone
But not for myself.
I even had to turn down
An opportunity I wanted to take,
Because I knew it took away
From the goal of balance
In my personal life, and rest.
I'm still recovering from burnout
From the last few weeks,
The last few months,
From the last few years.
I cannot take on more
That takes away from myself,
Even though I know I *can* do anything,
It doesn't mean that I *should*.
When at the end of the day,
I'm crashing and I can't even
Catch myself.
I choose me,
Even when the world tries to
Demand that I choose it.

<u>What We Do for Love Pt. 1</u>

I would fall on the blade
Of any sword that opposes you.
I would sell all my belongings
I would pack up,
Release myself of obligations
That take me away from my family.
The last thing you'll ever see of me
Is the way I show up,
Show.
Up.
For you when love is present.

But what no one sees is how I will also
Face the fears that
Keep me from myself.
The insecurities that keep me chained,
The trauma that stops me
From being someone safe to be around.

In the name of love,
Not only will I face your fears,
Your oppositions,
And challenges with you,
I will face all that
Holds me hostage from myself
And from you.

<u>Something Someone Else Does that Brings You Peace</u>
<u>Pt. 2</u>

Your precise hands
Braiding my hair
Is a comfort only you
Can provide.
Not many people can touch my hair,
But you my sister,
Are a guardian of the spirit
That lives as an extension of me.
Those moments together
Trusting the process and
Your expertise
Are moments I remember what
Connection we have,
We always have.
I'll keep you steady,
While you blaze forward, and
I'll love you forever.

<u>Sundays</u>

Sundays are for soft clothes
And fresh pastries,
Tea or coffee
At your own leisure.
Moving as slowly or as swiftly
As you'd like,
There is no rush here.
You belong to the liminal bliss
That is just being and
Just existing however you wish,
Before the rush of the next week.

What Happiness is to You Pt. 2

Your golden strawberry curls
Have been the sight of joy
Even when they were just a
Halo of fuzz around your head.
Your laughter,
My sweet bean,
Can melt the sun.
By far, there is more life
In your eyes than
In any Ocean,
Forest, or City.
Watching you grow,
Learn,
And love others
Has been an adventure
That I am honored
To be a part of.

<u>What We do for Love Pt. 2</u>

I know you would fight for love.
But would you embrace happiness for love?
Sacrifice your relationship to pain
To embrace joy,
For love?
Would you put down the stack of
I've-got-to-prove-them-wrong's
And sit down to watch
Your sibling's favorite anime?
Would you take the time to cook a meal
Instead of meeting the deadline someone else
Told you was a priority?
Would you stop and celebrate
For love?
I know all the harshness you would face,
But what about all the softness?
Perhaps, it is the softness that scares you,
Not the hardness and coldness
That you're used to dictating your life.
So, tell me,
What would you do for love?

<u>Transition of Summer to Fall and How it Parallels
Our Own Aging and Changes</u>

The youth of Summer,
The robust,
The freshness,
The ripeness that Summer brings
Is what we all hope to live for.
But as the fruits have been picked,
As the lively greens
Deepen and nourish
The next round of maturing,
We arrive to Fall
Much more quickly than any
Of us had anticipated.
The Autumn brings in the
Harvest of lessons,
Of the veggies and the
Gourds that will
Hold us on through the Winter.
Fall brings us to letting go
Of all that we can no longer
Sustain because as life changes
So do we, so does our truth,
So do our needs.

<u>Comparison of the Eye Color of Your Lover to the Same Color of Things You Love</u>

Your eyes light up like
Dark rich honey when
The sunlight shines through them.
I'd drizzle your stare across my
Toast in the morning,
Sprinkling cinnamon for spice.
Your deep gaze adds warmth and
Sweetness where my life
Was cold and bland.
Let me cup your gaze in my hands,
Warming my fingertips, the way
My coffee does.
Your amber irises are my sunrise
When the night has been long.
Bring me your stare,
Let me find ourselves there,
Where you dance with me and
Nothing else matters.

<u>Wearing Your Heart</u>

Sometimes I don't wear my heart on my sleeve.
Mostly, it's tucked beneath the ribs that
Have held up against every beating.
But sometimes,
Sometimes,
I wear it on my fingertips -
My thumbs.
Little traces of it left
On every single piece of paper
On every empty pen,
On the keyboard of my phone.
Because what is she
If I never share the softness
I wish I didn't feel so adamant
About protecting from a world
That truly just needs more softness.

<u>What it Feels Like to Hate Something</u>

I seethe with heat
That threatens to burn me
From the Inside out.
What a destructive force it is to hate.
Blindly, I lead to retaliate,
Blacked out in the name of protection.
I've read there is love in hate,
And it took me a long time
To see the diamond in the coal.
Have you ever hated someone or something
Where love should have been?
Patriarchy,
Racism, Sexism,
Being destroyed by someone you
Loved more than yourself?
If love would've been there in the first place,
Or if it never would have left,
This would be a much different conversation.
Love and Hate are opposites
For a reason.
When I am face to face
With the hate listed,
I myself go blind.
My morals go out the window
To protect myself,
My loved ones.

It is a veil over the eyes
As you swing in the dark and
Where your blow lands
You feel justified.
But who are you really hurting in the end?
Is it them,
Or is it you?

<u>The Silent Observer</u>

Have you ever felt like
You could exist in any space
And no one else would see you?
Your presence invisible,
Your ears not there,
Hearing conversations around you.
I've sat in rooms,
I've been in businesses
Where I did not fit in
And yet -
And yet,
I blended in.
As if part of the scenery,
As if I was the plant in the pot
Observing life passing by.
I've gained knowledge,
I've heard gossip,
I've seen private conversations
Take place where they should have been
Exactly that, Private.
Still, no one sees me.
I am here,
Taking it all in.
Waiting for the day
That all this invisibility and knowledge
Come in handy.

<u>I Don't Want My Soul Filled With Sugar</u>

I don't want my soul filled with sugar
Instead of salt.
I want it filled with honey and
Maple syrup.
There's depth in what those become,
A warmth and richness.
There is flavor there...
And if there's still a little salt,
It turns to baking.
So, in the morning I'm making waffles.

Spilt Milk

There is no use in crying
Over spilt milk,
But I spilled my coffee,
AND there's milk in it.
There's also inflation,
And my hours are
Getting cut at work.
So, I will cry over the
Spilt milk,
The waste of coffee,
The man I love
Being with someone else,
And the world being on fire.
I will bawl for the bones of
My ancestors I
Never got to meet and
Scream at the world
It isn't fair for the
Younger generations
Finding it so hard to live,
But I will still seek
Liberation for those of us
Who understand:
Living is meant to be an art form,
Not a life sentence.

<u>Tear me up Fam</u>

Tear me up fam,
I say as I see the proverbial
Wolf pack close in around me.
I can't run anywhere
I can't scream or
Fight my way out of this one.
The cycle that life leads
Has made its way back around
And this time,
This time
I have to just trust that
Somehow, I will make it
Out of this one alive.
Just when I thought I
May have to strike,
That the wolf may just pounce,
It stands upright and
Outstretches an arm
With a stone cold,
"Congratulations."

<u>Fragile as Fuck</u>

Fragile as fuck,
But not like the glass will break
If you tap on it.

Fragile as fuck,
But not like a flower that's
Crushed when you step on it.

Fragile as fuck,
As in if you step wrong
You're blown to smithereens.

Fragile as fuck,
As in I grew thorns
To protect the beauty I am.

Fragile as fuck,
As in I will crack to reveal
The fire within.

I will unleash your deepest fears.

So, watch how you love me.
I will make you
Or I will break you.

I Don't Want My Soul Filled With Sugar Pt. 2

I am not the sweetness that sugar
Rushes you to.
The obvious hello that you've come to know
As the flash of a smile and sparkling eyes.
I'm the slow viscosity of intimacy and trust,
An enveloping flavor that
You don't think of until you remember that
Sugar isn't the only thing that's sweet.
Honey, Molasses, and Maple Syrup,
They're all acquired tastes,
With a depth and richness that most
Stir away from.
I'm the bold lips that aren't here
To smile at you,
But to make a statement.
I don't mind being avoided until you realize,
There is no crash after me.

<u>Free</u>

I am free to be happy.
I am free to be heartbroken.
I am free.

A part of that scares me.
But that's okay.

Final Words

The happy moments in life
Are made that much sweeter
During the phases where life
Is unrelenting in its hardness,
Coldness, brutality.
Like the choking down of cough syrup,
The abrasive cleaning of wounds,
Or the snap of trees as they fall
To become something else.
Sometimes the sunrise
On a foggy morning
Brings you to tears with gratitude
For Still Being Alive.
Laughter brings you joy and stability,
As peace is looking around the room
You've fought so hard to call your home.
Sometimes the small things
Are your happy moments,
Until your happy moments
String together as the garland
You decorate your life with.

-Adriana O.

www.ingramcontent.com/pod-product-compliance
Lightning Source LLC
Chambersburg PA
CBHW021404160726
47994CB00007B/3075